His Mercy on the Disobedient

His Mercy on the Disobedient

Amber Rathof

Contents

Introduction 7

Chapter 1: Being Light in the World ... 10

Chapter 2: There Is Purpose for Your Life 21

Chapter 3: Serving the Kingdom 29

Chapter 4: The Joy of a Thankful Heart 37

Chapter 5: Prayer Life 46

Chapter 6: Faith Without Works Is Dead 52

Chapter 7: Mental Health 60

Chapter 8: The Key to the Spirit Realm 67

Chapter 9: Sin & Obedience 76

Chapter 10: His Mercy on the Disobedient 80

Chapter 11: Accountability 84

Chapter 12: Repentance 88

Copyright © 2024 Amber Rathof

Published by Amber Rathof

ISBN: 979-8-218-83454-8

All rights reserved. No part of this book may be reproduced or transmitted in any form or by any means, electronic or mechanical, including photocopying and recording, or by an information storage and retrieval system, without prior written permission from the author.

Scripture quotations taken from the Holy Bible, New International Version ®, NIV ® Copyright © 1973, 1978, 1984, 2011 by Biblica, Inc. Used with permission. All rights reserved worldwide.

Introduction

We often take the Lord's mercy for granted. I have been more than guilty of this. I have heard about how much the Lord loves me, but it took years for it to strike my core. I ran away from Him. I was a menace to society. I was fully soaked in disobedience and both fear and pride kept me from repenting on too many occasions.

I spent my days doing as I pleased knowing I could go to hell. I put my future in my own hands. And how many of us have done this? Thinking we had time, knowing that is a lie. I played god over my own life. I treated the Lord as if I had the power, not Him, to stay on this earth and decide when I wanted to do right. I thought to myself, *'Surely God won't do to me what He did to people in the Bible.'*

I thought I was untouchable, and I would somehow get away with sinning because God "wasn't doing anything about it." I treated His mercy like it was weakness, like He was made to be submissive to me, like I deserved to sin after all He let me go through. Looking back at where my heart was during my first book, I used my trauma as a shield, thinking it covered and excused my sins. I concluded, in my mind, I had a right to be nasty to people because people hurt me. It's easier said than done to be kind to others when they wronged you, or when you are hurting yourself.

Have you ever wanted to cuss someone out who did you dirty? How about if you have ever taken your rage out on people who reminded you of someone who hurt you? Like how you know the Bible tells you to be kind to others, but you don't want to. It feels impossible to get to a good place where you are able to live in peace. I was stuck in chaos. I wanted peace, but all I could see, and feel was pain.

I want to dive a little into different highlighted areas of ongoing growth. These are areas that we are to actively work on and practice in our walk with God. The Lord works on perfecting His children until the day we die and transition to be with Him. I have gone through so much in my life but so has the world. The Lord isn't some being that just sits high and looks down on us. He walks alongside us, although many times it feels like the opposite.

We were designed to worship and praise Him, to follow Him through Jesus, and to have an active relationship with Him. The

Lord is righteous in all that He does. He is our God, our Father, and our Friend when we need it. He gave us Jesus. He even gave us the Holy Spirit to guide us. Together, the three entities make the Trinity. And that Trinity is three in one: God.

As I go through new chapters of my life, I am learning more about myself and more importantly, more about the Lord. I pray that the revelation and wisdom in this book encourage you. Every person is a work in progress, so don't think you have to get it all together in a day, a month, etc. I wholeheartedly believe that life isn't worth living without the Lord.

Chapter 1:
Being Light in the World

Around the age of three is when I first became interested in God. There was this unexplainable desire in my heart to learn about Him. I wanted to know everything about God, too. I was obsessed with Him especially because I wondered what He was like. I wondered if He was like my dad. After all, I looked up to my dad. Dad held the position of being my favorite person. He had this title in my heart when he wasn't screaming at or beating mom. I looked at God as fatherhood, too. I just didn't understand fatherhood. I thought as a little kid it was bad to look at God like my second dad.

I started talking to Him as a toddler. I had this intense but calm feeling in my heart like someone was trying to reach me, so I began speaking to it. There was peace with it. I don't know exactly how it came about, but I learned to pray. I watched others talk to God and ask Him for things with their heads down. So, I practiced doing that myself sometimes. I learned to pray by doing this and when the Lord tugged on my little heart. I prayed for my parents often. God became a friend to me. I couldn't talk to or trust my siblings or parents, so I would take my issues to the Lord. I would say things like, "Please keep my mommy safe" and "Thank you for helping my family."

The Lord's work in the beginning years of my life reflected my interactions with my parents and adults. I spoke about things children don't understand. I knew things that were said in secret from adults. I was roughly three or four when I randomly said the word "encyclopedia." The Lord had put it on my heart to say. That word was not spoken to me before in my household. My parents responded with excitement, saying, "She is so smart!" I also heard my dad and a family member whispering about making dessert for us kids. They tried to be discreet, but I heard in my heart what it was. I said out loud, "It's a banana split." My family members looked shocked. "How did you know?" They asked. I shrugged, 'I just know." They were completely surprised and confused as they never said it out loud.

When you give your life to the Lord, His light is in you. The light brightens the darkness figuratively and spiritually. I have spoken about some of my spiritual experiences in my first book. I have a relative who told me a story of her seeing a demon in the hallway. She has similar spiritual gifts as I do. I will never forget her response when I asked how we are able to see these demons.

She responded, "The light in us brightens up the darkness. That's how we can see them. People who walk in darkness cannot see the darkness. Only those who walk in light." I unknowingly was learning to shine the light of God into the world. However, I was still confused and too young to understand the full extent of it.

Little toddler me learned to run around on fire for the Lord. I had this confidence when I spoke prophetically. I brushed off the rejection people gave me in response. Adults told me often, "You don't know what you're talking about." They also said things such as, "You don't understand." But I kept this strong desire to talk about God to everyone.

Starting in my teenage years and into young adulthood was when I had most of the backlash for talking about Jesus and God. This was a time when my parents allowed different people to come into our house. Some were family members with active addictions who were allowed to stay with us in exchange for pills, money, or rides. Some were friends who also had active addictions and were drug resources.

I spoke to some of these people as they came into our lives. One family member that stayed was initially receptive to receiving Jesus as opposed to everyone else. That's what I did. I straight up asked people, "Do you believe in God?" and "Do you accept Jesus as Lord and Savior?" I continued the conversation to ask why or why not. I encouraged them to give their life to the Lord.

As I grew older, I did this with men I dated. I even did this with coworkers. It felt impossible to tone down my passion for Christ. I did not understand the concept that I was planting seeds into people. I did not know that God was using me to draw people closer to Him. That light inside of me sometimes dimmed when I learned about what happened to the people I preached to.

The family member who was initially receptive to accepting Jesus quickly turned away from Him. She went down a dark road after her brother died from an overdose. She took off from our house that night as soon as she found out. Someone found her dead two days later in her family's kitchen. She also overdosed. To my knowledge, I was the last person to talk to her about Jesus.

It broke my heart as I wondered if she ever really gave her life to Him or repented before her last breath. I remember seeing an old coworker at a laundromat. We were not friends, but we were on good terms. She approached me and we made small talk. In the middle of our conversation, I awkwardly joked about plans I had and said, "If God stops playing." I wanted to talk about God some more but chocked up. I got a little bit out. Then an eerie feeling came onto my heart like something was seriously wrong.

Sadness fell across my face as I looked at her. *'She's going to die, isn't she?' I said in my heart.* I was scared for her as I knew she didn't know the Lord. I felt this sense of fear like there was no point in preaching the word because she will not turn to the Lord. Shortly after she left, I sat in my car and prayed. I tried to find her on social media but was unable to. Months later, I found out she had an active addiction herself and died from a drug overdose. One of the worst occasions was at an old job when a male coworker came in to deliver some things to us. I had just been talking to my female coworker about Jesus as He was on my heart again. She grew frustrated with me and yelled, "That's not the only way to heaven. My mom is a Christian, too. I know all about it."

The male coworker walked in, and I felt a tug in my heart to talk to him about the Lord.

I asked him, "Do you believe in God?" She snapped back instantly, "Oh my God. Leave him alone! He doesn't believe in God. Stop talking about this. Stop talking about your stupid Jesus!" I looked at him again, "No one has to believe, but do you?" I sensed a death for him. He and I both looked away for a second in embarrassment.

He looked at me quietly, saying "No I don't." My heart dropped and I said something like "You should. You could die like that and meet Him." My female coworker responded again, yelling, "Get out! Stop shoving Jesus down our throats. I'm tired of hearing about this. My mom is a Christian. I'm a Christian, too. Leave us alone!" I shook my head in resentment at her.

I glanced back over at him to look for any changes in facial expressions, but he remained standing still with a blank expression. "Get out!" she commanded and shooed me out of the way by waving her hand away. As I closed the door behind me, I could hear her flipping out. She was saying, "I'm so sorry. I hate when she does that. I don't know why she does that. Please don't talk to her!" I paused, looked up at the Lord, and said, "I tried." He died like six months later. His father passed away, and he put a shotgun in his mouth.

A man I dated was angry when I asked him about God. He had lost a child, and to my ignorance he was angry with the idea of God taking his child. It got to a point where he shoved me and cussed at me. "I hate you! I hope you die!" He yelled. He also had a drug addiction.

Even though I knew enough to desire to talk about Jesus, I was still considered a "babe" in the faith. I barely went to church. I had a connection to one church that I went to on and off, one night a week as a kid for children's activities. Sometimes, I walked over as a teenager and young adult for service on Sunday.

I wanted to know everything about Jesus and God so I could have a response for every question or opposing view. It upset me that I couldn't respond or defend the Lord in most of the conversations I had. It took me years to learn that not every opposition needs or deserves a response. I learned that you cannot force people to believe in God let alone accept Jesus.

We, disciples of Jesus, are the salt of the earth. We are in this world, but not of this world. The world doesn't know God. They do not understand how He works and operates. People treat God like they do humans. People turn away from God because of other humans' behaviors. It's easy to dismiss what you don't understand. People often go through tragedy and grow angry towards God. We don't know or fully understand why God would allow people to die or suffer. His thoughts and ways are greater than ours, but that truth doesn't always make it feel better.

The Lord tells us to be bold. This is important when spreading the gospel or showing the love of God. God's version of love consists of attributes like patience, kindness, not envying, boasting or being full of pride, keeping no record of wrong doings, not getting easily angered, or self-seeking. When you don't feel like being that light or you are hit with fear, boldness (in addition to the Holy Spirit) helps push you through.

People sometimes can't see the Lord through us if we are too afraid to be bold and shine our light. I felt scared many times talking about God and allowed myself to back down on a couple occasions. It grieved my heart during those occasions because in the moment, I felt the spirit of fear come on and I held back. After I missed the opportunity, I would hold my head down and apologize to the Lord. Sometimes I felt so bad for messing up I cried my heart out to God.

As I develop into my walk and relationship with Him, I still speak boldly about things He says. I try to recognize when my passion is okay or when I need to tone it down and take a different approach. I get excited to talk about the Lord and what He has done for me. There are moments when the Lord will tell me not to speak, or He will tell me to walk away.

I like to tell people what I am believing God for, too. Because I sometimes get anxious and forget the world doesn't know Him like I do, I must remember to obey the Lord's voice and approach things as He guides me. I cannot expect someone else to rely on faith even though I know the power of it, and even though I know what God can do. I can tell people I am trusting God for something and declaring His Word and let them witness His goodness.

God will raise someone up to be His light. You never know who is watching you. You especially never know who you might inspire or lead to the Lord. God knows your entire life from start to end (more accurately from the end to the start) so He will give you opportunities to shine. We, the children of God are taught to walk in biblical truth, which stands against things society likes. But it is things such as these that draw people to

God. The Lord will work on perfecting His children until the day we transition to be with Him.

I realized later in life how my ability to shine the light of God was always conditional. I had put my dad on such a high pedestal that it set me up for failure. I knew, even as a small child, dad had so much potential. He was going to get sober and become a pastor someday. He was very smart, gifted, and talented. Regardless of how bad his addiction was, he made the effort often to remind us how much he loved us. To me, being the light was only talking about Jesus and what He did. I was missing an extremely important piece to this: showing the love of God. As I grew up, the anger I felt towards my parents grew with me. I ran around preaching to everyone, but I wasn't authentically representing the Lord.

I was not patient or kind. I was quick to respond and get angry. I was jealous, self-centered, and competitive. I spent my days spewing mean things to others and getting defensive all while putting a label of "Godly" on it. I lashed out on people the Lord led me to talk to because I was having a bad moment. When mom or dad upset me (usually mom), I complained about it and put the spotlight on me instead of serving the person as I was called to serve.

This is why I talk about the significance of my parents' death. Until a man leaves his parents and come together as one with his wife (vice versa), the parents will remain as the head of the family. Having two very broken parents who were unable to be the motherhood and fatherhood I needed kept me distracted. After their passing, the Lord renewed my heart and mind. He gave me a new purpose to live.

My heart was open for God to come in and be my new dad. Having a new Dad who loved me greatly and would never have an addiction or hurt me, who instead healed my shattered heart. With the Lord as my mother and father, I started practicing being a light to the world in a whole new sense. I was now showing the love of God with a new perspective. I sometimes struggle, but with my Heavenly Father I can think of and pray more for others, even those who hurt me. If you are feeling down, like you may never get to show the love of God, remember He works all things out for the good of those who love Him, who have been called according to His purpose (Romans 8:28 NIV).

Chapter 2:
There Is Purpose for Your Life

God created you with purpose. He created you with a plan for your life. He created you to worship and trust Him. He created you to fulfill His purpose on this earth through assignments, trials, etc. Before He formed you in your mother's womb, He knew you (Jeremiah 1:5 NIV). You were more than some clump of cells created from an interaction between your mother and father.

He knew every struggle you would have. He knew every choice you would make from start to finish before you came down to earth. He knows every hair on your body. He counts every tear that you shed. He created mankind altogether for purpose, too.

This is why the world hears about people being against things such as abortion. The Lord had placed purpose in those unborn children before He even put them in their mothers' wombs. I understand that this knowledge takes a jab at many hearts because the world as a whole has a difficult time accepting that there is a God, and He is greater than anything we can ever imagine.

I have come across the same questions when it comes to death and bad things. When my newborn brother died, I wondered why. I was devastated and angry at the Lord. When my older brother died of cancer at 32, I had questions, too. One of the biggest challenges was wanting and trying to give answers to my sister as her six-week-old baby died in her arms. I don't know the reasoning and purpose that the Lord had behind these tragedies. I have my own ideas, but again God's ways and thoughts are much higher than ours.

What I love about the Lord is that there is room at His table for every single person. The Lord takes your personality and your testimony and can use it to expand the Kingdom of Heaven. You and I may have similar stories and testimonies, but there is a crowd of people in this world I can reach that you cannot and vice versa. There are people you can reach that I cannot and may never. But you must be willing to be used by Him because He does not force anyone. He is a gentleman and gives every single person a choice.

Sometimes, He reveals how He wants to use us later in life and sometimes it's early on. I was five years old when the Lord told me I would be an author. However, even at that young age I still wanted to fulfill my own desires. I had no idea how this would play out, though. I wanted to practice writing books but did not know what I was supposed to write about. Eventually, I had written four unpublished books of my own before I was a teenager.

These books were all handwritten. I had written my first one around the age of 7. This one was a shorter story of around maybe 20 sheets stapled together. This one also included a prophecy that my dad would die when I would be 25 or 26 (I was 26 when he ended up passing away). I had given this to a family member around that time, so I don't remember much of the story line off hand.

Two of my books were childlike romance stories, each consisting of about 30-40 composition sized notebook pages. I was around 11-12 years old for both of these. My most prized story was one full composition book plus another half about a supernatural experience. I lost it over the years, but the story remains in my heart. Someday, I would like to re-write it. This special story was written over a couple years during my preteen era, and I finally finished it by 13.

And it was in my teenage years that I was bullied at school so badly I felt useless. I felt like I served no purpose for existing, like I was better off gone. Writing stories, songs, and poems, drawing, or doing some type of craft helped bring me back. I consider them part of my love language. It helped remind me that there was more to life than bullying and my parents' addictions. Having dealt with those things, I can see that purpose is connected to tragedies, trials, and tribulations. I believe that my parents' deaths were necessary to help me give birth to my purpose. When mom and dad were alive, I was stuck in chains of bondage. I was stagnant in my walk with the Lord. I was able to push myself through college, but I wasn't walking with the Lord like I wanted to. I had the desire to draw closer to Him, but not the discipline.

I love my father, but his decisions helped leave me with a hardened heart. I was in heavy bondage because of this. I had daddy issues and surely would not turn to God for fatherhood. The Lord introduced me to men who represented the fatherhood He designed man to be. He even allowed other men to enter my life as lessons. However, I perverted nearly every single relationship I had with men. I gave myself away for attention and short-term love if I could.

It never filled the empty void, but I continued to repeat the cycle. I have always desired a husband and children and desired to create my own family for the Lord. However, I was not ready in any area for that kind of commitment. God values the family unit deeply. He knew I would have destroyed my marriage because of my daddy issues. I chased older men to make up for the lack of love I felt from my own dad.

Then there was my relationship with my mom which was a whole different kind of bondage. Between her own narcotic addiction and legit health issues, I could not escape her grasp. She leaned on me for everything. When I moved out, she continued to ask for money, food, and rides. I just wanted her to love me. I wanted to be a good daughter because I actually thought I was a terrible daughter when I did not do something for her.

Because of the dynamic in our relationship, I did not know what motherhood was either, I only knew how to be a parent to my parents. She would take from me, multiple times a day. I felt like I was in quicksand. I could not get out of it. I was mentally tired. I tried to numb the pain with food and sex. I was angry at her for not doing better. I was angrier at myself for being angry at her. Her health issues broke my heart. I knew she was struggling, but I still wanted to be free of her.

I have had a few years now to reflect on my relationship with both parents. They made their choices. The Lord gave them so much grace and mercy to repent and choose life. I was even angry at my brother Justin because, when his life was in my hands, it felt like I was chained to mom all over again. I do not know why bad things happen. But I do understand that my tragedies were what opened the door for the Lord to reach me. If everything is going well for you, you might not have room for your relationship with the Lord to grow. After all, how can you know that God is good, and that He will get you through the storm if you don't go through any storms?

Sometimes your purpose can be found hidden underneath the tragedies you went through. It's one thing to have read the Bible and be able to quote it. It's another thing to have lived through it and have the revelation to confirm the truth of the Bible. The Lord does not say He will get us over the problems and avoid the process. He promises to be with His children through the fires. With mom and dad being in heaven, I can see spiritually clearer. I can also accept and understand trials better. Their battles played a role in hindering my purpose, but I am still accountable for my choices.

I encourage you to come to the Lord and surrender it all to Him. I encourage you to reset your mindset, too. Nobody wants to suffer. We all fall short before the glory of God. However, what you go through can help lead someone else to the Lord. That is the purpose for all mankind - to expand the Kingdom of Heaven. It's not always about us. It's about riding it out and getting through the storms. It's about long suffering. And when the dust settles, you can receive the revelation as to why you went through that storm. You can then use that testimony to glorify God.

You have the free will to come to God's throne boldly, repent, and keep trying to do His will and obey His assignments and His word. He will shape you and give you the desires of your heart through the process. You are not a waste of life. You matter. You are so valuable, more precious than anything this earth and Satan can offer you.

Everyone has different assignments and God's plan for their life typically is unique and tailored. If you're like me, you could have started receiving pieces of your purpose as a toddler. Sometimes, it takes people most of their life to learn theirs. The Lord will reveal it to you and sometimes send people to confirm it for you. Seek the Lord first.

Chapter 3:
Serving the Kingdom

The Bible is filled with many verses about serving. It mentions things like iron sharpens iron and not withholding good from someone who deserves it when you have the power to act. After all, Jesus Himself did not come down to the world to be served, but to serve. Another verse talks about how the servant is the greatest among you. Also, we weren't called to use our freedom to indulge, but to humbly serve others.

At this point, it would be good to mention that there is also not one kind of serving. Serving can include your time, money, or talent. For years, I thought the only real serving was what people did in church. I even had my heart set on doing the most at my church. I served in three different ministries at one point. I worked every weekend but made a commitment to making sure I served at least one of the two services on Sundays.

I felt discouraged when I did not get recognition. I felt ashamed when I taught Sunday school and leaders would come in and observe for a moment. I was ashamed that I wasn't the most exciting teacher or making a difference. I got nervous. I wanted to stop serving but pushed through for the Lord. Unfortunately, I stopped completely when dad died and have struggled with consistency since then.

The problem was that I wanted to be praised for everything I did. I wanted to be put in the spotlight each time I picked up a shift in one of the ministries. And I was angry that others were praised when it appeared like they did less. I had a problem doing things in the moment for the Lord. I made serving all about me. But God loves a humble servant. I, on the other hand, was selfish. The Bible says those who exalt themselves will be humbled and those who humble themselves will be exalted. This is what was happening. I exalted myself to a level I felt I deserved, and the Lord kept me at the bottom to be humbled.

When it came to serving others, my opportunities were mostly my family. But I was greedy with my time and money as well as my resources. I had many chances to serve my family for the Lord, but because of my resentment towards them and their behavior, I refused many of those chances. I wanted everything for myself. Because of everything

I endured in childhood, I felt they didn't deserve my help most of the time.

The Lord will work on perfecting you until the day you transition to be with Him. He will put His desires in your heart. He worked on my heart as I kept messing up. I tried to serve the church again but kept quitting after a short period of time. I became more willing to serve outside of the church because my heart was still hardened.

I have no idea how I have gotten to this point other than knowing it was the Lord's work on me. I would be lying if I said I stopped struggling with serving the church. When I started to really grow in my walk with the Lord, I began to understand the concept of obedience to him. I started to understand the importance of really doing His will and placing myself in positions to practice serving others and showing the love of God (one example being serving at church).

It's true that the spirit is willing, but the flesh is weak (Matthew 26:41 NIV). My spirit was willing to serve, but my flesh kept getting in the way. Honestly, I continue to struggle because of my pride, anger, and resentment. People from church have hurt me throughout my life. It hardened my heart. I resented the body of Christ because I felt too many were phonies and nasty. I have also often been too proud to want to serve. I understand that the first will be last and the last will be first, but my flesh sometimes still craves acceptance and attention.

My flesh sometimes would rather be the main character than one of the background people making it all happen. There are moments where the Lord puts in my heart about serving again and getting back in routine with doing so. In those moments, I am willing and ready until the time comes, and I change my mind and turn away. This kind of selfless serving that God asks of us is essential for the Kingdom of Heaven. It also teaches many people how to serve and prepare them for their assignments (whether you are assigned in the church or the world).

I am aware that my assignments have been in the world. However, that doesn't mean I am exempt from being used by God in the church. God will use you to reach people, you just have to say yes to His will. Imagine how worse off the world would be if people didn't give their time, gifts, talents, and resources. Churches have individually and collectively been a blessing to society on all levels. Sometimes when there is a need for something like food, clothes, or rental help, churches have come together to support the needy.

People who receive the support might not remember the names of the helpers, but they will remember the name of the church. Imagine if more of the body of Christ was like me in my flesh, filled with pride and selfishness (If I am being honest with myself), instead of pushing down those fleshy issues and doing for God despite how I feel? Makes you wonder how many others will not get to see the love of God and the body of Christ in unity, representing Jesus as a whole.

Because of the Lord, I am more willing to be used by Him. I actively try to study His Word to show myself approved unto God. As for serving with your money, I absolutely believe in the law of tithing. The Lord has put it on my heart to tithe to my church during the periods when I refused. I was financially struggling and had no desire to wait on Him. I wanted an easy fix to my mistakes.

Still, I obeyed Him and paid my tithes. Serving with your money isn't just relegated to church. He will also tell you sometimes to pay for someone's gas or coffee, or even hand people money. Some people will be called to use their cars to pick up a neighbor or someone they don't like to help them get to and from work. There are so many ways to serve others. The Lord expects this, but he is gracious and merciful when we refuse to do so.

What I learned is that serving has nothing to do with your feelings. You cannot stop serving just because you don't feel like it. You must push through. Your willingness to do so is not in vain. God sees your press. However, your reward can either be from people or from the Lord. Galatians 1:10 (NIV) brings up the point that if we were trying to please others, we would not be servants of Jesus.

I like the verse that mentions "not telling your left hand what your right hand is doing (Matthew 6:3 NIV)" It helps keep my paths straight when I get the urge to boast on my good deeds. I see videos and posts from people bragging about the good they have done. If we are honest, I have done this many times myself through my own life. The Bible says when people do this, they have already gotten their reward (and it wasn't from God).

When you serve others, it is better to get your reward from heaven. You might not get the recognition you feel you deserve, but the Lord sees what you do in secret and His reward is greater than any attention or praise you can get from people. Remember in addition that faith without works is dead. Overall, God designed you to serve others for Him and to serve Him. If you choose to trust the Lord, this is essential to your relationship with Him.

When the Lord tells me to do things, or He puts desires into my heart, if I obey Him and fulfill those assignments, I am practicing faith backed up by my actions. I am not only trusting Him, but I am also intentionally making choices to obey Him and show that I trust Him. For example, I struggled financially, which is like most of the world. Like I said earlier, I had no desire to tithe. I needed that 10% of all the money I received to help with my debt. I can use that money for other things instead of giving it to my home church. However, if I trust God truly, then I should be obedient to His Word.

I know I will be fully debt free some day in Jesus' name. Even though it doesn't look like it will happen anytime soon, I continue to tithe and wait on Him until the time comes. This is faith with works. The concept of serving is absolutely tied to faith with works, too. I encourage you to practice trusting the Lord, learning to hear and obey

His voice, and serving for Him and His glory, not yourself. It's not an overnight change, but you will overcome it in Jesus' name.

Chapter 4:
The Joy of a Thankful Heart

God's will for us is to give thanks in all circumstances and rejoice. We are to give thanks because He is so good! When I reflect on and remember all that He has done for me or gotten me through, I feel so grateful. The Bible tells us things such as to enter His gates with thanksgiving and His courts with praise.

Praising the Lord and keeping a thankful heart go hand in hand. I had an issue with both for the longest time. I knew He deserved to be praised and thanked, but when times were tough or my feelings were hurt, I didn't want to thank Him. I chose to be ungrateful and bitter in most responses. Even at a young age, I knew acting like this was wrong.

Our flesh is weak, so it makes sense in our humanly minds to not want to be grateful to an almighty God because something didn't go our way. Our flesh is selfish, self-seeking, and self-serving. I battled one tragedy after another. I did not understand the bigger picture. I prayed for years for my father to get sober and turn away from the addiction. I also prayed for my mother to be better.

In my first book, *Grace in Resilience*, I talked about how my dad would scream at and beat on my mom until 2 or 3am every single night. He also beat her often during the day. He blamed her for everything. I had just prayed for my dad again to get sober a night or two before when dad was in one of his moods. He did not hold back from letting us witness the chaos. He beat her in front of us much of the time.

He got in her face around dinner time this one night. He pulled her hair and punched her in front of us as we were eating. I tensed up as my body filled with anger, then ran upstairs and locked myself in my bedroom closet. I was terrified. With me being one of the oldest, I often tried to intervene and yell at him to stop. It was like he was demon possessed. He would have this evil and hateful look in his eyes. I prayed and pleaded, but when he got like this, nothing stopped him.

I hid in my closet crying and hitting myself. I grabbed one of the random flip phones lying around and called 9-1-1. The cops showed up and mom and dad changed character. Mom came looking for me to get me to talk to the cops but gave up after a few minutes. I tried to hide well enough that she could not find me. After the cops left, I heard the door slam and dad holler, "Where is she? I'm going to beat that piece of crap!" Dad was verbally and physically abusive to us, too, just not as often as mom.

He came upstairs, found me, and yanked me by my hair out of the closet. "Why the hell would you call the cops you fat pig?!" He screamed and proceeded to punch me repeatedly in the head, face, and arm. Mom pleaded for him to stop beating me. He stopped after what felt like a dozen blows. I hid back in the closet and hurt myself again. After he was done beating me, he stomped down the stairs cursing me out the entire time. Before leaving, mom too turned to me and said, "You deserve it for calling the cops!"

"I effing hate you. I don't believe in you no more!" Ten-year-old me cursed at God. I was so angry that God allowed stuff like this to happen. This same scenario happened a handful of times more, and only a couple times was I able to escape dad's beating. Unfortunately, if dad didn't beat me, mom did in his place. She would scream things like, "I hate you! Why did you call the cops? He's already in a bad mood. It's all your fault! I hope you die, you ugly pig!" She would hit me upside my head as well as dig her nails in my neck or arms, pull my hair, and use hard objects to beat me with. As you can see, I had so many reasons to be mad at God and withhold gratitude.

I hated my life. I was poor, surrounded by addicts, and cornered by chaos. Nothing seemed to be going right. Nothing seemed to be turning around. There was not even a glimpse of light I could see at the end of the tunnel. How am I supposed to thank God and show gratitude, when He has given me nothing but grief and pain? How can you trust God that things will get better when there is barely relief for the everyday battles? You wake up with emotional distress and go to bed with it. And the cycle just keeps repeating. But somehow I am supposed to lift my hands up in praise and show God how grateful I am? I didn't want to. The bible tells us that in God there is peace, but why can't some feel it for more than a few moments?

It's hard to see the positive when you only know the negative. People would try to encourage me and lift me up in spirit, but that ended instantly the moment I had to come back to the chaos of my own home. Any light that was in me was sucked out the moment my foot stepped inside the living room.

I prayed for my dad to get clean and instead he dies from a drug overdose. I prayed for my mom to get better and overcome this really bad stroke she had and instead she goes septic and dies. I prayed for my newborn brother to live and instead he dies as a stillborn. I pray for my older brother to beat cancer and instead he dies from cancer. I prayed for my premature niece to overcome her health issues and instead she dies in her mother's arms from those health problems. I even prayed for God to take my life, and He didn't give me that. I prayed for so much and so many things throughout my life. To those who don't understand, these would all be reasons not to be grateful to God but let me explain further.

Yes, the Lord allows bad things to happen, but those bad things are only on a temporary basis. And really, those bad things are mostly rooted in choices we make in our humanity. He will return one day for His people. The Lord honors His word. I encourage you, despite how you feel, to keep a thankful heart knowing that this suffering on earth is temporary. One day, He will call His children home and the bad things we experienced on earth will no longer be remembered. I learned to trust Him with my own life because that is all I can control. I learn to pray and trust Him with my family's lives as He knows better. I reflect on my parents' choices as well as my own.

Yes, my parents made awful choices. Yes, tragedy hit my family and me in ways that don't make sense. But I am held accountable for my responses, and my own actions – not God. Regardless of the pain, I have so much to praise God and be grateful for. God could have let me die when I was consumed by own sin and anger. Like when I was in the middle of committing sin, He could have easily removed the Holy Spirit from me, judged me, and allowed something bad to happen to me. But He does not go against His own Word. God forbid the bad thing led to my death and, in this case, I would have been separated from God and gone to hell. God takes forgiveness seriously and commands us to forgive others as He has forgiven us.

I have pointed my fingers at my parents and persecuted them for the years of suffering I have endured. But then the Lord showed me in return, "What about your mistakes?" He commands us to honor our mother and father. I have disobeyed and dishonored them so many times. God sees every single sin as equal. I am thankful for the opportunity to have helped lead my mother and brother to the Lord before they transitioned to heaven. I am thankful that God had so much mercy on my father, and they had a relationship even when he died from drugs. I am also grateful that babies go to heaven because I know my brother, niece, and every baby aborted or miscarried in the world will never see hell.

There is comfort in Jesus' words when He said to let the children come to Him because the kingdom of heaven belongs to ones like them (Matthew 19:14 NIV). Jesus has also told us that those who take the place of a little child is the greatest in heaven's Kingdom (Matthew 18:4 NIV). It's a reminder that although they are born into sin, children are humble and innocent.

I am grateful for God's grace and mercy on my life because I have a chance to get to heaven. Not only do I get to heaven, but I have family up there ready to reunite. I am especially grateful that I grew up with both parents. I could have been on the streets or in foster care because of my parents' actions, but the Lord kept me with them. I had things to be grateful for during the storms, too. He walked with me through those storms. He made ways for me to get out (sometimes I didn't listen and rerouted the path). When the dust settled and the storms calmed, I received the revelation of why I went through the storm. I received peace during and through the storms. He kept me fed and clothed. He gave me so many days of life and new chances. So yes, there is a lot to be upset about, but the good that He has done for us is greater than the bad things we endure.

He even made a way for us to restore our relationship with Him. He gave us Jesus and absolutely nothing compares to that alone! I have seen where Jesus was hung, laid down to rest, carried the cross, and where He performed miracles when I traveled to Israel. The God I have gotten to know is a good Father! He is a great friend in need.

As I mentioned earlier, He is both motherhood and fatherhood when I need it. He is also almighty God when I act up and He has to put me back in line. I battled with motherhood and fatherhood issues my entire life. I put too much stock into people. God allowed these bad things to happen not because He wants to see me suffer, but because these heartaches would help shape me into the woman of God He has called me to be. You see, He provides a way of escape with every trial and temptation. Because of my trials and tribulations, I trust God more than anything.

If I were to be persecuted for belonging to God, or if I were to live until old age, whatever the case may be, I will praise Him and give thanks until the last breath I take. Thankfulness and praise are preparation, after all, for heaven. This is what all of creation does in heaven - praise Him. Whatever happens in my life, whether it be self-inflicted, some type of disobedience after God warned me, or something I had no fault in, I trust Him with my life. Being grateful and giving Him praise is the least I can do!

Chapter 5:
Prayer Life

When it comes to prayer, it must align with the Word of God (the Bible). The Lord is not moved by emotions. The Word encourages people to come (all who are weary), and He will give you rest. The Word also says we are more than conquerors. However, God is not a genie where He will sit around and just grant our wishes.

The concept is to come to the throne boldly, that we may get mercy and grace in a time of need (Hebrews 4:16 NIV). We are to humble ourselves and keep a humble walk. We are to declare the Word over every situation. This is specific for those who have received Jesus. An example is when my brother got a terminal cancer diagnosis. I needed to remember that God has the final say, not man. We do not discredit the doctors and medical staff. We thank God for them, but the concept is to trust God through the Bible. God has the final say, but you must give Him that power over your life. What I did was declare my family members healed, whole and healthy. I thanked and praised God as if my prayers were already answered. I trusted that God's will be done.

So, when my relatives transitioned to being with Him, I trusted that this was His will for their lives. This is why it's so important for us to learn the Bible. The Bible is difficult to understand from your flesh. I encourage you to pray for the Holy Spirit's guidance and assistance when praying and reading the Bible. I learned that being in the spirit (Holy Spirit led) made it easier for me to receive the messages from the Bible.

The Lord wants us to pray for everything and everyone. We pray as a way of talking to him, building our relationship, and stating our needs. Prayer invites the Lord into our problems and our lives. He doesn't need our prayers to help us, but it's our way of including Him. He wants to be all in our business. After all, He does know best. But He gave us the free will to choose, and it makes Him happy when we choose to ask Him for help or talk to Him instead of relying on our own doing.

He wants to be completely involved in our lives because He adores us that much. I imagine He would love for us to even pray while using the bathroom. Unfortunately, many people like me fall short when it comes to praying. I, for one, like to look at Him more on a friend level where I don't always speak my prayers (sometimes out of laziness) because I know He can hear and knows my heart. I sometimes fall short when I get lazy or forget that I still do need to speak the word and prayers out of my mouth, too.

I sometimes get lazy and don't declare the Word. I sometimes get caught up in my emotions and only after I finish crying will I declare the Word. This isn't a bad thing as the Lord wants this. Now, don't think that someone is more saved or better than you because they praise and pray in a certain way. Religion is different than relationship with the Lord, and the world does not know this. The world thinks that presenting yourself in a certain way, never making a mistake, and doing the most good deeds are things that make you saved.

God is not looking for who appears and speaks the most sanctified. The world looks at outward appearance, but God looks at the heart. Remember He already knows what mistakes you were going to make, and He offered you mercy and grace on it (through Jesus). He already lined up a way out through every one of your messes. Rather, He is looking for authenticity. I talk to Him like I would like a great friend. And I try not to curse (praise God for the day I overcome it!).

The Holy Spirit is crucial to your entire life, not just your prayer life. As I mentioned before, the Lord comes as a Trinity. There is God the Father, the Son (Jesus), and the Holy Spirit. If willing and obedient, the Holy Spirit will guide you on what to do, what to pray, when to pray, what part of the Bible to declare, when to stop talking, when to speak, etc. The Holy Spirit is literally there to live and walk this life out with you!

You ever wanted to do something bad that you knew you shouldn't? And when you wanted to do that silly thing, did you have a friend telling you not to do it? Maybe you thought, 'It won't be all that bad.' Maybe your friend appeared to exaggerate what could go wrong. But imagine you listen to that friend and afterwards, you get hit with the realization that your friend just saved you from disaster. That's what it's like to have the Holy Spirit go through life with you. The Holy Spirit is an extension of God Himself. He knows everything. He knows the hearts of every single person. He is there to keep your focus on the Kingdom of heaven, to keep you out of harm's way as needed, and keep you on a straight path. He is committed to you for life as long as you're willing.

Also, when it comes to your prayer life, remember it is not on your timing but on the Lord's. The Lord is not bound by time. He doesn't have a clock sitting next to His throne in heaven. He is not slow to move, either. We live in a society where people have short attention spans and want everything answered and completed in the snap of a finger. God talks about the importance of patience, but the world wants the opposite. The world in general goes against the Word of God. When you pray, wait on His timing for an answer. You can have an answer in minutes or centuries. In other cases, your prayers might not get answered and something else happens instead of what you prayed for. God will even wake you up at random times to pray or give you an answer. I know as I was writing this book, the Lord would sometimes wake me up at 4am to give me directions for what to write.

In addition, declaring His Word/praying helps keep you focused in the spirit. This will help keep you away from sin. You will still sin, but I learned that being in the spirit helped keep my mindset straight. When my flesh wants to do things such as gossip, curse, or speak badly about someone,

I noticed that being in the spirit and hearing from the Holy Spirit made it easier for me to recognize when I felt like sinning or temptation was approaching.

Pray for all things and worry about none. Leave it in the Lord's hands.

Chapter 6:
Faith Without Works Is Dead

This chapter is somewhat of a continuation from my previous chapters. God Himself knows what you need during each battle, season, or situation. He already prepared our pathway to conquering these battles and transitions. As I briefly discussed in previous chapters, I struggled with mommy and daddy issues deeply. I had this expectation that my parents should know better, so I set unrealistic expectations for them. I criticized their mistakes, even small ones such as forgetting something. I wanted them to do better. I resented them for their choices because it negatively impacted me and my siblings. Alcohol and drug addictions can turn you into something you never wanted to be. Not one person is exempt from bad things happening to them let alone changing them.

I know the Word of God says to honor your parents. This is commanded from the Lord because it represents God's order and respect for His authority. Parents are intended to be a blessing and have authority over their children just as the Lord himself is a parent with authority over His children. Parents are above their children in God's order. This only changes when the son or daughter leaves their parents to marry and then the marriage is the start of a new family.

I wanted to follow this command, and the Lord put that desire in me, but I was stuck because their actions and choices angered me, and that anger and lack of honoring felt justified. I trusted God for them to be better. I prayed and believed. And I couldn't understand why God allowed my dad to die from a drug overdose. I didn't actually want my mom to die either, despite part of me wanting it because of the suffering we had been going through for so long. I didn't get the answers I was hoping for. It felt like honoring my parents and intimately walking with God only applied to others, like it was unreachable for me in my situation.

My hardened heart assumed that somehow those people must be liked by the Lord more than me since things are working out for them while I experience the opposite. Now, as I walked this earth bitter and angry, God still stood by as a friend. He still showed me kindness and gave me reasons to smile.

The Trinity still had my back when I walked away from God.

There is God the Father who created all things. There is God the Son who came down to earth as Jesus who is the only way to get into heaven by the way. You can spend your days trying to be a perfect and good person, but none of that matters in the end if you don't have a relationship with Jesus and/or if you did all of those good deeds for you instead of God.

The Holy Spirit is the third part of the Trinity. The Holy spirit is literally the Spirit of God. He will speak to you. He will prophesy to you. If you have a prophetic gift like me, He will do things like show you visions or give you prophetic words to speak to someone. You will know it's the Lord if it comes to pass. God's word, whether it be the Bible or a prophetic word He gives someone, will never come back void. They always come true.

. I battled with trusting the Lord because of the bad times. I would pray, believe Him for the prayer to be answered, thank Him sometimes, and then feel empowered. However, when a bad moment of trial and tribulation came, it was as if I never believed God to help me. I would fall back into doubt.

I would grow angry with the Lord and frustrated at the lack of "answered prayers." In my mind I wondered how I was supposed to trust Him for a better life when all I see is darkness. I wondered when this nightmare life would end.

Life wasn't getting any better. I didn't want to die, but I wanted it to end, and death seemed to be the only way the pain would stop. The Lord was already prepared and kept me alive. He got me through those moments of despair. He got me through the wave of emotions and guilt I felt during and after any attempts.

The Lord can move mountains even if your faith is the size of a mustard seed! He assigns angels to assist you. Angels can do things like fight the spirit realm on your behalf. They can assist you with arriving somewhere safely. They serve the Lord, and He assigns them to serve us for His glory.

It was only recently that I began to see the Lord in a different sense. With my parents now in heaven, I had this desire for new motherhood and fatherhood. And I still need it to a degree. I said before how I looked at God as another father figure. I prayed for great motherhood and fatherhood in place of my own natural parents. I absolutely trusted the Lord and believed in Him for this to happen. My job was preparing and believing for it. My faith came in when I gave it to the Lord and moved on as I trusted Him to bring me new motherhood and fatherhood when He said it was time. A while later, the Lord actually took the place of my parents. He is the greatest form of it ever and no one can even come close. Afterall, the Lord is a Father to the fatherless (same with motherhood).

I have come a long way with disobedience in this area, too. I still sometimes battle with wanting to act on rebellious behavior. God does not like disobedience. But His love for me as His child struck me and my heart felt convicted. It made me realize 'Hey, this is how a father is supposed to love their child.' God isn't just a father, but He deserves and earned the title dad and daddy. He doesn't deserve a rebellious daughter. He deserves an obedient daughter who trusts Him to know what's best for her and her family. He broke the hard shell on my heart, and I let Him in. I was resistant to doing so because I was afraid that He would be like my own dad. The only fatherhood I had known up until this point was my own dad. I wasn't there yet with knowing God for who He is. I didn't know yet what kind of Father God is and how very different He is compared to my own dad. However, when I think of and speak to the Lord, I feel loved, wanted, and special.

God is perfect. He is just in all His actions, decisions and judgement. He takes sin very seriously, but He also has so much love for His people that He will help them through it. In my earthly dad's arms, I was left vulnerable and scared. In God's arms, I am safe. This broke chains of resentment, anger, and bitterness. This true love from my Father in heaven has changed my heart. I want to please my Father. I want the world to know how amazing He is.

It hurts my heart to see people reject Him because they don't know Him and the enemy is deceiving them. I trust Him with my life. I could lose everything, and the most important thing is that I don't lose the Lord. I told him I do not want to live a second without Him. I don't deserve Him, but I absolutely and desperately need Him.

I trusted the Lord through most of my life with faith the size of a mustard seed. And when I doubted Him, and He stayed. He removed things and people from my life I thought I needed and gave me greater. He took my earthly dad, and I got Him instead.

He took my brother and replaced Him with Jesus. He removed people from my life that I wanted to hold onto. He gave me the Holy Spirit who provided companionship when I needed that, too.

Even when your relatives are alive, the Trinity remains in those roles. God doesn't just become your Father because your dad is alive. He was, is and will always be your Father. Jesus isn't only your brother when you lost your own. Jesus was, is and will always be your brother and your family. It's not just the orphans and widows who need the Lord in these roles. It's the folks with a full family alive and well who need it, too. There are people who have what I lost and are hurting just as much. This family unity from the Lord is for anyone who wants it.

Things did not work out anywhere near what I hoped for, but He has shown me that what He can do and give me is much greater than anything I thought I wanted. This revelation has led me to actively try and be more obedient. It opened my heart to His rebuke, and instructions. I was more open to feedback and accountability.

God has had to rebuke me often because I still give into my flesh and get off track and into sin. I trust God so I am now receptive to His rebuke. I am also learning to include Him in everything, even politics. I want my Father's input and guidance on every single part of my life. Have I gotten there? No. He will work on us until the day we transition to be with Him. I have learned to truly trust God when I could never trust my parents. That revelation alone makes me smile. I have the best Father AND I can trust Him 1000%?! Wild. I am more willing to do His will. He has helped me so much with this book.

When you obey His voice, do an assignment He has called you to do, trust Him through the process, take steps to help fight your battles as He tells you, obey His warnings, repent when He rebukes you, rebuke something in Jesus' name- stuff like this is what counts. Doing works with faith is what He wants. Remember that being obedient to Him is faith with works, too.

Chapter 7:
Mental Health

I am very familiar with battling mental health challenges. I believe almost the whole world deals with mental health battles to some degree. I want to say my social work background has helped me greatly with recognizing issues and practicing tools to help me get through my own problems. The Lord graced me to go to college and get a master's degree in social work. It helped me shape my perspective on things from the natural realm that we see. As a Christian, I believe that mental health battles come from the spirit realm. There is a spirit behind all things such as depression, suicide, and anger. If the enemy can attack your mental health, he can keep you away from the Lord. He can shift you down a dark path that leads many to death. I was diagnosed at 30 years old with bipolar, PTSD, depression, and anxiety.

If you physically look at or talk to me, I believe it's generally evident. I get overstimulated daily which triggers anxiety. However, the anxiety comes from multiple different things. Even though I trust God, I still haven't fully overcome the PTSD part. I still sometimes struggle with hanging on to the past and allowing the pain of it to hurt me. I continue to battle family issues that trigger me. People sometimes behave in a certain way, and it reminds me of the negative behavior of my parents. I struggle with consistency in areas because of the highs and lows I deal with. The bipolar disorder will have me super energized and on top of the world for a minute. Then, just like that, I lose all energy and desire to do anything. I get depressed and doing simple tasks becomes difficult.

I had mentioned in *Grace in Resilience* how my brain turned off like someone hit a switch and it would cause me to shut down. I believe it's linked to bipolar disorder. When this happens, it's like I can't even function normally. I would be lying if I said I mastered this part of my life. Truth is, I am learning to seek God's help and fight in Jesus' name as the battles come. This is a hard topic to discuss because there is creditability in the natural realm. There are resources for people to seek such as support groups, hotlines, and therapy. All resources have made differences in people's lives. These resources bring positive results. I do not discredit resources like these because I understand the importance and value of them.

I encourage others to seek these resources even though I struggle with utilizing them myself. My mental health has impacted my relationships with people. People walk away because of my anger and short temper. Sometimes, I am too much for one person to take in, so they walk away because of that. It has also negatively impacted my assignments for the Lord. When I am in a low, I refuse to do some things for God because I get lazy and unmotivated. It has seeped into every area of my life.

On the opposite end, battling these mental health issues has helped make me sensitive to the world. It has even helped me recognize things in others that most people overlooked. The Lord will meet me in my struggle, and work in me because of it. If my life was perfect and I never struggled with these issues, there wouldn't have been room for God to help me. God shows me He will get me through it.

What has worked for me was pleading the blood of Jesus or declaring His name during these battles. One of my greatest examples was when I went to church to see a guest prophet coming from out of state. I came home afterwards and laid down to reflect on my relationship with the Lord. I felt this overwhelming spirit of fear hovering over me. It felt like there were multiple people surrounding me at my bed egging me on to kill myself. I had no thoughts about suicide, yet here I was suddenly drowning in this push to do it. It was heavy, like something was weighing me down to do it. I had to declare the name Jesus and rebuke that spirit of suicide.

The world rejects the truth of the spirit realm. People have been convinced that life is only what you physically see and that supernatural experiences aren't actually real, that people who believe in God or the spirit realm have mental issues. I have been called schizophrenic by heathens. Having a conversation with someone is difficult when their heart is hardened, and they are unable to see a perspective outside of their own.

Since depression has been a familiar spirit throughout my life, I learned that the name Jesus is what helps me rebuke that spirit. His name delivered me from that spirit. Unfortunately, when you have struggled with some of these spirits for so long, you will need deliverance multiple times and a lot of spiritual warfare to help rebuke them permanently. When these spirits have taunted you for so long, they don't always just go away. Another great tool to battle mental health is being in the spirit. This happens when I am praying, praising and worshiping the Lord, hearing from the Holy Spirit, etc. I can hear the Lord clearly. It's like being high on the Holy Ghost.

I can refrain from sin because I am focused on the Lord. My flesh is better controlled. The more I stay in the spirit, the better I can handle my mental health. The world of medicine is so advanced it offers medications to help with mental health, and those aren't bad. However, nothing has helped me more than the name Jesus and being in the spirit.

I also want to note that I recognize we live in a time where mental health is being used to excuse poor behavior. It's being used as an entire personality for some. The whole world is claiming they have anxiety. I believe a great number of people battle it. However, the issue with this is when people hyperfocus on mental illness. People are in bondage because of mental health battles such as identity, anxiety, depression. I experienced my own battle with identity as a teenager. I dressed as a tomboy most of my life because I was insecure about my body, and it was comfortable. After being molested at 12 years old, I questioned if I even wanted to be a girl anymore. I thought if I transitioned to a boy, I would be safe.

Of course everyone's battles and reasonings are different, but the Lord did deliver me from this. Having mental health issues has been more widely accepted as an illness (and that's great progress), but the world is struggling to appropriately handle it. Unfortunately, the enemy has people focusing on themselves and competing for who is more mentally unwell than the next person. Additionally, the enemy has people questioning who they are.

People are being fed all of these lies like saying God "made a mistake" when some people were created. The Lord intentionally and purposely designed you male or female. He gave us instructions on how to act and live through the Bible. Yet, the enemy is running around trying to deceive and lie to people. The enemy is telling people things such as, "God messed up. This is not who you truly are;" or "The Bible is old school. God gave you free will so be whoever you want to be."

The best version of you is who God intended you to be. And here the enemy is convincing people to live in their flesh and give in to their own desires – that is sin and goes against God. There is such a high demonic attack on the mind and some people wonder why mental health has become such a popular thing to promote instead of being treated. Those demons taunting you don't want you to get better and seek the Lord. They want you to self-destruct through feelings and emotions, challenging God's design.

The enemy has demons throwing these thoughts into peoples' minds about how they should commit suicide. He tells them that they aren't supposed to be the gender they were born, that God messed up when He created them. The enemy makes them think that their family who talks about Jesus and cares for them are actually awful people who don't want them to be happy. All it takes is one second of entertaining that idea or dwelling on it to allow it to grow in the mind.

The enemy has people isolating themselves. The Lord will call people to help deliver others from these battles, but the enemy will try and swoop in to get people isolated so that God's people can't reach them, and God can't deliver them. The demonic spirit realm is working overtime to keep people in their own mental bondage in the hopes they don't turn to the Lord. The enemy doesn't want people to learn the power of the name Jesus. He doesn't want people to break free from the bondage.

Chapter 8:
The Key to the Spirit Realm

In addition to mental health, declaring the name of Jesus and pleading the blood of Jesus have been the most powerful tools to combat the spirit realm altogether. I have seen and heard the spirit realm my entire life from hearing the Holy Spirit to looking at a demon in the eyes. I have astro-projected. I have seen hell in a dream. I have seen a couple of demons as well as heard the voices of many.

I understand how crazy that sounds to others, but I absolutely believe in the spirit realm. It's a separate realm from this natural, seen realm that we live in. I believe the closer we get to the return of Jesus, the more these two realms will collide in a sense. It's not a coincidence that people are having more supernatural experiences. It's even more of a non-coincidence that people are having dreams of and coming to Christ.

Every knee shall bow, and every tongue will confess at the name of Jesus

(Philippians 2:10-11). One of the biggest battles for me regarding the spirit realm was sleep paralysis. The world recognizes it but denies its true definition. This is a very spiritual experience. Sleep paralysis typically happens while you are sleeping but can still occur when you are fully awake.

You will feel this spirit of fear over your body. You feel paralyzed, unable to move. You can't breathe. It can feel like you're being suffocated or frozen. I have experienced this a couple of dozen times over my earlier years. I found it occurring more when I was fully awake as opposed to sleeping.

One of the scariest moments was when I was interning at a school. It was the end of day, and I was looking for a restroom before I left. The adult ones were all taken, so I went to the girls' bathroom. I was alone in the bathroom and after a couple of minutes, I heard a knock and someone creek the door open. I heard a man say, "Is anyone in here?"

I started to speak but got a slight mumble out. "Hello?" He asked. It felt like I lost my voice, like something was suffocating me enough to stop me from speaking. I felt that same paralyzed feeling. I couldn't move. The man called out one more time before proceeding to lock the door. As soon as he locked the door, I started crying out, "Jesus."

I couldn't say His name entirely. I had to keep fighting to say it. I started out saying "Jee" then "Jees" until I eventually got to "Jesus." Once I said His whole name, I kept saying it until I felt the release. Once I got my feeling back, I called one of the staff members I was shadowing to get security to let me out. The security guards were visibly irritated. The man who called into the bathroom happened to be one of the two guards that came.

I told the staff member later about what happened. Thank God she was a Christian too so she could understand what happened. This is why it's so important to pray for people (not just family or friends, but enemies, too), schools, jobs, churches, etc. This school was for grades kindergarten through eighth grade. Young children walked in these halls as demons carried out attacks. I witnessed multiple demonic acts at this school. I have felt demons crawling on my bed towards me before episodes of sleep paralysis happened. People have stories of seeing demons at the end of their bed or in their room. Anything the world may offer as a solution can't even come close to the power of the name of Jesus.

In addition to this, demons and Satan will try to set traps to deceive you into thinking something was of God. I had always heard from the Holy Spirit yet found myself overthinking about it. This caused me to seek His voice. I laid down on my bed one night and locked the door so no one could come in.

I sighed, and said out loud, "Lord, I am here if You want to speak." I laid completely still for a few moments before that familiar feeling returned. I once again felt my body get numb, like I was paralyzed. My legs became too heavy to move. I heard a loud, audible voice in my right ear. It was like a loud whisper, but I couldn't understand what it said.

"Lord, is that you?" I asked. I then felt myself lifting off the bed. I knew something was off. I cried out the name, "Jesus" and felt myself come back down. I felt a little frustrated with the Lord as I was hoping to hear His actual voice. I wondered for a while if that was Him or a demon. When it's the Lord, there is no confusion. It took me a lot of thinking in the Spirit before I connected the pieces that this was demonic.

God does not change who He is (Malachi 3:6 NIV). He is the same yesterday, today, and forever more (Hebrews 13:8

NIV). The world thinks God changed because the world did. But the God of the Old Testament is still the same God in the New Testament. The enemy has taken what God established as a practice for the remission of sin and copied blood covenants. Behind closed doors, the enemy has people making blood sacrifices and blood contracts to elevate their status. I have heard and I believe the testimonies. People were told in order to get fame and fortune they had to make a blood contract with the devil and "sell their souls."

However, none of us own our soul. God does. People will secretly sacrifice newborn babies or random strangers to the devil to try and gain something they want like defeating old age or death. The enemy will take things that the Lord does, twist it, and abuse it to deceive mankind and convince them that they can play God and control their outcome.

I have no doubt that there are people in this world drinking the blood of others with the belief that Satan will give them longer life and all the money they desire. Satan knows that God loves humans very much and is forgiving. But God is not one to be mocked. Someone can do this ritual thinking they defeated nature and God, and the next day God will take their life. Now they are spending eternity in hell and there is no reset button.

Movies will tell you there are alternative ways to defeat demons. I have seen movies where they read a bunch of pages and do some kind of ritual to get rid of demons. The Bible is clear, there is no tool greater or more powerful than the name of Jesus! If the enemy can get you to watch and believe these movies and television shows that promote alternative ways, he can get you away from using the real tool: Jesus.

Another big copy I want to speak against is fortune tellers. I have fallen into this trap of going to see an individual typically in a dimmed room with tarot cards and other kinds of witchcraft laid out. You pay a fee for them to seek your dead relative or tell you about your future or specific situations. This is highly demonic, not of God, and a copy of God's gifts, one of which is the gift of prophecy.

I have a prophetic gift. The Lord will give me dreams, visions, and prophetic words. He will talk to me about and show me my issues or future battles as well as others. My job is to obey the Lord in these moments. Sometimes He wants me to tell someone the dream I had of them. Sometimes, He wants me to speak the prophetic word to whoever it was for. Other times, He wants me to just listen and pray for the person or group.

God wants us to do things for His glory, not our own personal gain. The idea is that we do things for God, and He will reward us. God takes obedience in this serious, too. So when I see fortune tellers, my heart grieves. Most of them don't know better. I believe some of them do have prophetic gifts but are misusing and/or misunderstanding those gifts. The individuals who do not have this gift or are misusing it are being demonically influenced. There are familiar spirits who hang around and watch us in the spirit realm.

They study what our flesh likes and what we struggle with, and they use our weaknesses against us. Demons have attacked me in dreams after my parents died. When this happened, I cried to God to stop letting the dreams of my mom happen because they hurt. These familiar spirits know that. So when a fortune teller tells someone there is a dead loved one they miss, of course they can give some details. There is a demonic spirit inspiring them with those details.

It is appointed for man to die, then after the judgement, you will either go to heaven to be with the Lord or hell because you rejected Him. Sometimes it's comforting for people to believe that no one goes to hell, that people just stay in limbo. Or that when you die nothing that happens. This is a lie. This has people believing they will never be held accountable, nor will they need to be because "nothing will happen after death."

The enemy has people believing that nothing occurs after death, yet somehow, it's possible for aliens to exist and your dead loved ones to visit you. See how he tricks people? There is evidence of God all around us, but the world is taught to overlook that and think it's just a made-up religion to keep people in bondage.

Everything in this seen realm is a reflection of what happens in the spirit realm. God created mankind and the earth from the spirit realm. When you are going through something, understand that it reflects a battle in the spirit realm. So when you plead the name and blood of Jesus, you might not see much happening in this realm but know that the power is hitting that unseen realm.

And pleading His name is not a waste! Same thing applies to praying. Just because it doesn't physically look like anything is happening does not mean you did it in vain or that it was a waste. You will see the results from the unseen realm come into your view at some point. Stay encouraged. Remember there is no greater tool than the name, Jesus.

Chapter 9: Sin & Obedience

The concept of obedience has always been something I heard about but had no revelation on it. I spent my days running away from God like Jonah. Sometimes, I felt too far gone to bother trying to obey the Lord. I had committed sin so many times, I thought my grace period expired. I often felt the tug at my heart pulling me to come back to the Lord.

I would feel inspired and try but within the first couple of days I would get stuck again. My resentment towards my parents seeped into every single area of my life. It impacted my ability to learn obedience. I was running rampant with disobedience. I had two sick parents who struggled to set rules and limits. If nothing serious happened, then we could pretty much do whatever we wanted.

God takes sin very seriously. In His eyes, all sin is equal. The world cherry-picks which sin to call out. The world says it's not okay to steal, but it's okay to have sex before marriage. God sees every single sin as bad as the others. Someone stealing a pack of gum is just as sinful as someone committing murder.

The Word of God confirms that all fall short before the glory of God (Romans 3:23 NIV). Any sin can separate a person from God's grace. Isaiah 59:2 (NIV) talks about how our sins create a barrier between us and God, preventing Him from hearing our prayers and needs. For example, If I hang around people who gossip and slander others when I don't gossip myself, it might seem okay at first.

Even though the Lord is against gossiping (James 4:11 NIV), I can control my tongue, right? Eventually, little moments may come when I start to gossip, but I am still able to catch myself. This continues until those little moments become more often and eventually turn into a full conversation of gossip. Now, I am in trouble with the Lord.

This is what all sin does. It may start in small occasions, but it opens the door for the enemy to get in. It leaves the door cracked for more sin to come through until the door is all the way open and you are covered in sin. Anything against God's will, whether it feels big or small in your eyes, is equally an issue to the Lord. I fell into the lie that I can sin all day every day and God will forgive me at the snap of a finger if I choose.

In my heart, my parents loved me conditionally. Therefore, I didn't want God to control my life just for Him to love me conditionally, too. I saw God as I did my parents. I did not respect Him. I resented Him for putting desires in my heart to change for the better. I had a prophet tell me one time, "God loves you, and love requires action." But anything that made me think of my parents caused something in me to want to rebel. We can preach until we are blue in the face about how much God loves us, but until someone receives the revelation of His love, they could likely sit stagnant. You can only plant seeds.

Idolatry is another issue that hindered my obedience. I was super obsessed with fleshy things like sex and chasing money. I did not want to sacrifice these self-seeking things in order to please God. I wanted my cake, and I wanted to eat it, too. I knew by getting closer to God, I would eventually have to change my ways and give these fleshy desires up. I was disobedient to the Lord when I struggled with gluttony, and when I disobeyed and disrespected my parents (even though their actions played a part in my rebellion). I knew better regardless, and my obedience was up to me to maintain, despite how others treated me. We can't control someone's actions, but we can control our own. The idea is that each day when we wake up, we are to actively deny our fleshy desires, try to stay in the spirit, being Holy Spirit led in everything, and repent as often as we sin.

Consistency falls under obedience, too. However, please note that believers benefit from God's mercy. We cannot be sinless, but we start to sin *less*. You can't be obedient one day then get all into your fleshy desires the next. God gives grace and mercy, but He is not obligated to, and He can and will judge you if you keep committing those sins deliberately. Picking up your cross and walking with the Lord is a day-to-day battle. You must practice consistency. The Lord does not like disobedience. He expects you to be obedient.

Consistency, therefore, comes when you practice obedience. You might have to take it one minute at a time. It will likely be a daily challenge to pick up your cross and follow Jesus in the beginning, but as you push through and make the effort repeatedly, it eventually becomes easier to do. This leads to consistency. You can get to a point where obedience comes natural to you like waking up or eating a meal.

Chapter 10:
His Mercy on the Disobedient

I can preach for days on how much the Lord has spared my life from going to hell. Not only does God offer mercy and grace, but He will also let someone be consumed by their own sins. He does not desire for this to happen, but He allows it as this is the result of the person's will instead of the Lord's. I absolutely deserve to be in the depths of hell! The sins I have committed, the people I have hurt that I never thought I would, what I have done to gain those couple of moments of satisfaction - I do not deserve an ounce of mercy. God gave me mercy when I was nasty to others, when I gossiped about people, when I destroyed my own character and someone else's, when I cursed, and when I set a bad example to others who looked up to me. God is very just in His judgement. God is perfect, and righteous in all things He does.

There were times when I was consumed by my own sins. I remained stuck like this for so long. This is when the Holy Spirit often tugged on my heart to come back.

God owns our bodies, our souls, everything on this earth but God is not obligated to keep you alive. Each day that you wake up is a blessing. God may be giving you another day to repent, to do His will, and/or some other type of purpose. It's a hard pill to swallow, the fact that we are not in control of some things such as the Lord waking us, but I am grateful that He did so I have another chance each time to re-do it.

God knows your entire life from start to finish. He knows who would turn to him and at what point. He assigns angels to people who belong to him as well as those who don't give their life to Him until a later time. God even knows the thoughts of your hearts before they come to mind. God is all knowing and all powerful. I don't know why He kept me alive when I acted unsaved my whole life. But here I am, still here and still getting chance after chance to try again. He still has given me mercy. This is where religion misses the mark. Religion had people like me in bondage.

In my earlier years, I believed that people who never did things like smoke, drink, or miss church would make it to heaven and the ex-cons would go to hell. The world teaches you that flawed people shouldn't be in leadership or give testimonies. But how can you lead people to Christ if you don't have the revelation or testimony of what He can do? How can a perfect and "flawless" person preach to a bunch of sinners? Only Jesus had this position of being a flawless preacher. This is why we should not look up to anyone or try to mirror anyone except Jesus.

However, there are individuals that can represent God the correct way. Even though no one comes close to Jesus, we cannot exclude the people that do the will of God. You study the person by looking at the fruit that they bear as a result of operating in the fruit of the Spirit. The fruit of the Spirit are characteristics that show that someone walks with the Lord. This fruit consists of peace, gentleness, patience, kindness, and self-control.

It's also important to have discernment where you can recognize subtle or lowkey things that the average person might not see. That's why there are phrases such as "wolf in sheep's clothing" You cannot simply dismiss people who don't look the part of saved and sanctified. You also cannot just accept anyone who "looks" holy. If someone is lacking the fruit of the Spirit, pray for them. The Lord may have you minister to them, too.

God saw your sins beforehand. He planned an escape for each one ahead of time, too. He allowed some things to occur so that He can deliver you and teach you to trust and rely on Him. He has given us mercy, not so we can keep sinning, but to get delivered. There is no other reason I am here other than God. He has a plan for my life, and His mercy carried me to this season full of wisdom. We must remember not to grieve the Holy Spirit, either.

Grieving the Holy Spirit occurs when someone disobeys the Lord and commits sins or actions that hurt their spiritual growth. We must study to show ourselves approved unto God, a workman that needs not to be ashamed, rightly dividing the word of truth (2 Timothy 2:15 NIV).

Chapter 11: Accountability

Accountability was never my strong suit. It was never practiced in my home, nor did I grow up around people who openly demonstrated it. I watched my parents dodge accountability and blame everyone else for anything that went wrong. In turn, I learned to copy their behaviors. I refused to accept that I was wrong or made a mistake. I avoided questions and deflected the blame on someone else (even when there was evidence against me that I messed up). I felt stuck in this way of life. That still, small voice (the Lord) pulled on my heart to do the right thing and take accountability, but I was struggling to apply it.

My heart grieves when I remember how awful my behavior was in previous jobs, schools, etc. God was good to me and often gave me leadership that dealt with me through my mess. People didn't want to be around me (understandably). I was nasty, mean, anxious, and stubborn. I had this chip on my shoulder like someone was always out to hurt or wrong me. As I grew into my teenage years, I started shifting all blame to my parents. Although their actions did cause a lot of ongoing issues for me, I blamed them for things I did that they didn't even know about. Like when I mismanaged my money, and my car broke down after giving my mom money, I would blame her for not being able to pay to fix the car.

I ran away when I was called out over something I did. I stormed off when someone wanted to have a simple conversation with me. I refused to engage with people who spoke to me about anything that didn't revolve around me being a victim. I was self-centered and wanted the attention only on me. I resented being held accountable for my parents' actions. The fighting was constant and, in my mind, taking accountability meant it was my fault things went wrong. I blamed myself for their addiction. I blamed myself for their fighting constantly. But when mom passed was when I let God in this part of my life.

Because of that newfound freedom, I wanted to change my life for the better. I recognized that I had this problem and gave it to the Lord to help me. He allowed me to be in situations sometimes where I made a mistake and was called out on it. For the most part, I accepted any consequences and took accountability. We don't 100% change overnight. We have a lot of baggage for the Lord to work through. As the Lord helped me do better in this area, I began to think about how the Lord works. When every single person dies, and judgement comes, we will all be held accountable for our actions both good and bad. This gave me the revelation that God knows and sees everything.

With that being said, how can I do a disservice to myself and never practice accountability while on earth knowing I will have to face it for real before the Lord? Who am I hiding from when the Lord is who I must answer to and give an account to? On another note, we are required to actively try to avoid sin and take accountability through repentance when we do sin. This plays a big role in how I present myself now. I try to remain open and honest. I have often overshared things about myself. I adopted this mindset that if I remain open and honest, people cannot say I am not taking accountability for things. We are a work in progress. Accountability is very important in general.

Also, the lack of accountability is a generational curse in my family, especially on mom's side. So praise God if He raises you up to break that curse because the lack of practice leads many to destruction. You might get away with people not finding out, but you will never get away with it when it comes to God, and He is the one who will hold you accountable in the end. He is the righteous judge.

Chapter 12: Repentance

I have briefly mentioned throughout the book that the Lord created mankind to worship and serve Him, and to have a relationship with us. To recap (in case anyone is not aware of the back story), sin started when the Lord created Adam and Eve. They were in the garden of Eden where they lived perfectly in relationship with the Lord. The Lord told them they could eat fruit from any tree except the tree of knowledge of good and evil. A serpent appeared and tempted Eve to eat from this forbidden tree. Eve did eat the fruit, and gave it to Adam who ate it, too. This was the first sin and led to the fall of mankind.

Due to Adam and Eve's mistake, all of mankind from that moment on is now born into sin. For God so loved the world, he gave his only son so that whoever believes will not perish but have everlasting life (John 3:16 NIV). God gave us Jesus. Jesus was born onto a virgin named Mary. Jesus walked this earth as the human form of God. Jesus is the only perfect human to ever exist, and He was sin free. He is the example of how we are to live.

Sin is a perversion of what God designed us to be. It broke the covenant we had with God. This is why He gave us Jesus. Jesus is now the covenant for God to have His relationship back with humans. However, each person has to be willing to accept a relationship with the Lord. That relationship means changing your desires to be more like Jesus, like who God created you to be.

The world preaches a false narrative where you can believe in God and still hold onto your sins. The world lies and says you don't have to change who you are, that God will love you and accept your sin, and you have "time" to get right with Him. The truth is you can die tomorrow and it's only God's grace that wakes you up each day.

When I look back on my life and think about the dumb stuff I did that hurt the Lord, I am grateful that He has kept me here and alive. I absolutely deserve to go to hell for the sins I keep committing. But God has been merciful and has graced me each day to try again. He has given me so many chances to do the right thing.

Repentance plays an extremely important role when it comes to having a relationship with God. Repenting is honestly acknowledging your sins to the Lord, turning away from sinning (actively trying to), learning to have a new understanding of your behavior that leads to the sin, and knowing that the Lord will then wipe away your sins and gives you a clean slate.

This is an ongoing thing for the rest of your life on this earth with the Lord. Not repenting is a dangerous thing. People have believed the lie that they can repent later and are okay enjoying their sin now. What if the Lord removed you from this earth before you had the actual chance to repent? It would be too late. There is no certain time or location where you are to repent or pray for that matter. You are to do so as needed. I have said before that the Lord continues to perfect us until the day that we transition to be with Him.

God requires us to love as He does. The world's version of love is conditional based on the person's feelings. God's love is extended to all, regardless of who they are. The Lord remains right there, ready to take you in with mercy that renews each day. Plead the blood of Jesus against any bondage you may have that is keeping you from accepting His grace or continuing to sin. I pray that you receive from this book revelation on and can attest in your own life

God's love and His mercy on the disobedient. Amen.

www.ingramcontent.com/pod-product-compliance
Lightning Source LLC
Chambersburg PA
CBHW071227160426
43196CB00012B/2439